Life in the Early Islamic World

Science, Medicine, and Math
in the Early Islamic World

Trudee Romanek

Crabtree Publishing Company
www.crabtreebooks.com

Life in the Early Islamic World

Author: Trudee Romanek
Publishing plan research and development:
 Sean Charlebois, Reagan Miller
 Crabtree Publishing Company
Editor-in-Chief: Lionel Bender
Editors: Simon Adams, Lynn Peppas
Proofreaders: Laura Booth, Wendy Scavuzzo
Editorial director: Kathy Middleton
Design and photo research: Ben White
Production: Kim Richardson
Prepress technician: Katherine Berti
Print and production coordinator:
 Katherine Berti

Consultants:
 Barbara Petzen, Education Director,
 Middle East Policy Council and President,
 Middle East Outreach Council;

 Brian Williams, B.A., Educational
 Publishing Consultant and Editor.

Cover: Artwork of an Istambul observatory in 1577
 (center); A page from the book *The Compendious Book
 on Calculation by Completion and Balancing*, written by
 the mathematician Muhammad ibn Mūsā al-Khwārizm
 (bottom left); Avicenna's statue in Dushanbe, Tajikistan
 (bottom right)
Title page: An Astronomical Observatory (Jantar Mantar) in
 Jaipur, Rajasthan, India, built by Maharajah Jai Singh II
 in 1727–1734

Photographs and reproductions:
The Art Archive: 9 (University Library Istanbul/Gianni
 Dagli Orti), 11 (Topkapi Museum Istanbul/Gianni
 Dagli Orti), 13 (British Library), 14 (National Library
 Cairo/Gianni Dagli Orti), 17 (University Library
 Istanbul/Gianni Dagli Orti), 22 (Private Collection/
 Marc Charmet), 23 (Topkapi Museum Istanbul/Gianni
 Dagli Orti), 27 (Topkapi Museum Istanbul/Gianni
 Dagli Orti), 32 (National Museum Damascus Syria/
 Gianni Dagli Orti)
shutterstock.com: 1 (Angelo Giampiccolo), 3 (Orhan Cam),
 5 (ayazad), 6 (J van der Wolf), 8–9 (Ajay Bhaskar), 15
 (Tyler Olson), 24 (Voyagerix), 28 (shao weiwei), 28t
 (M.Khebra), 29m (I.T.), 30 (javarman), 40 (Alberto Loyo)
Topfoto (The Granger Collection): 12, 26, 31, 34, 38, 39,
 42, 43; (World History Archive): 18, 19, 21, 34–35;
 (Luisa Ricciarini): 23, 33; 36 (Roger-Viollet), 41
 (The British Library/HIP)
Wikimedia: cover-center (Cahiers de Science et Vie No114),
 cover-bottom right (Alefbe), cover-bottom left (John L.
 Esposito. The Oxford History of Islam. Oxford
 University Press), 37

Maps:
Stefan Chabluk

This book was produced for Crabtree Publishing Company
by Bender Richardson White.

Library and Archives Canada Cataloguing in Publication

Romanek, Trudee
 Science, medicine, and math in the early Islamic world / Trudee
Romanek.

(Life in the early Islamic world)
Includes index.
Issued also in electronic formats.
ISBN 978-0-7787-2170-3 (bound).--ISBN 978-0-7787-2177-2 (pbk.)

 1. Science--Islamic Empire--History--Juvenile literature.
2. Medicine--Islamic Empire--History--Juvenile literature.
3. Mathematics--Islamic Empire--History--Juvenile literature.
I. Title. II. Series: Life in the early Islamic world

Q127.A5R66 2012   j509.17'67   C2012-900283-6

Library of Congress Cataloging-in-Publication Data

Romanek, Trudee.
 Science, medicine, and math in the early Islamic world / Trudee
Romanek.
 p. cm. -- (Life in the early Islamic world)
 Includes index.
 ISBN 978-0-7787-2170-3 (reinforced library binding : alk. paper) --
 ISBN 978-0-7787-2177-2 (pbk. : alk. paper) -- ISBN 978-1-4271-9840-2
 (electronic pdf) -- ISBN 978-1-4271-9563-0 (electronic html)
 1. Science--Islamic Empire--History--Juvenile literature. I. Title.

Q127.A5R66 2012
509.56'0902--dc23

 2012000077

Crabtree Publishing Company

www.crabtreebooks.com   1-800-387-7650

Printed in Canada/102013/MA20130906

Published in Canada
Crabtree Publishing
616 Welland Ave.
St. Catharines, Ontario
L2M 5V6

Published in the United States
Crabtree Publishing
PMB 59051
350 Fifth Avenue, 59th Floor
New York, New York 10118

Published in the United Kingdom
Crabtree Publishing
Maritime House
Basin Road North, Hove
BN41 1WR

Published in Australia
Crabtree Publishing
3 Charles Street
Coburg North
VIC, 3058

Contents

About This Book

Islam is the religion of Muslim people. Muslims believe in one God. They believe that the prophet Muhammad is the messenger of God. Islam began in the early 600s C.E. in the Arabian peninsula, in a region that is now the country of Saudi Arabia. From there, it spread across the world. Today, there are about 1.5 billion Muslims. About half of all Muslims live in southern Asia. Many Muslims also live in the Middle East and Africa, with fewer in Europe, North America, and Australia.

Science, Medicine, and Math in the Early Islamic World looks at the important ideas, discoveries, and inventions made by Muslims and related scholars from the 600s C.E. up to about 1800. It shows how their work influenced other peoples and our everyday lives today.

In the Beginning

Muhammad was born at Mecca in Arabia about 570 C.E. He heard messages he said were from Allah, **or God. Muhammad became the** prophet **of Allah, and founded the religion of** Islam. **His teachings changed history.**

Muhammad the Bedouin

In early times, most people in Arabia led hard lives. They were Bedouins of the desert and believed in many gods. They lived in family groups called tribes. They were **nomads**. They moved from place to place to find water and food for themselves and their animals. Some tribes were **allies**, but others often fought and raided one another. This led to more fighting, with revenge attacks.

Muhammad belonged to the Quraysh tribe. He traveled the desert routes as a merchant. He believed the tribes should live in peace. He believed that rich people should share with the poor, but saw that many Arabs were not living this way.

In 610, Muhammad told people of messages he said came from God. The messages told how Arabs should live. In 612, Muhammad began preaching to others. Some people followed him, to worship and pray. The world had a new religion—Islam.

Timeline

570 Muhammad born in Mecca

610 Muhammad tells people of his first message

622 Muhammad's followers leave Mecca for the town of Yathrib (later called Medina)

630 Muhammad returns to Mecca

632 Muhammad dies

651 **Muslim** armies conquer lands that include Syria, Palestine, and Persia

651 Islam reaches China

661–750 Umayyad Caliphate (series of caliphs, or leaders)

750–1258 Abbasid Caliphate

929 Abd al-Rahman III becomes caliph in Cordoba, Spain

1050 Islamic Empire expands into Africa

1055 Seljuk Turkish leader seizes Baghdad

1096 First Christian **Crusade**, or holy war, begins

1143 *Quran* is **translated** into Latin

1171–1250 Ayyubid Caliphate

1193 Muslim rule in Delhi, India

1281–1324 Osman I establishes the **Ottoman** state in Anatolia, Turkey

1453 Mehmed II conquers the city of Constantinople and renames it Istanbul

1632–1654 Taj Mahal built in India

1918 Ottoman Empire ends after Turkey's defeat in World War I

Below: This black building called the **Kaaba** is in Mecca. It is Islam's most sacred shrine. It is surrounded by the world's largest **mosque**—the Masjid al-Haram. During the **hajj**—the annual pilgrimage to Mecca—millions of Muslims flock to the Kaaba.

Geographical Spread

Muhammad set out to set up a new state under the banner of Islam. He and his followers won battles even when they were outnumbered. By 632, Muhammad had control of Mecca and Medina, towns important for trade and religion. Most of the people in the region were now Muslims (believers in Islam), or had made peace with Muhammad and his followers.

After Muhammad's death in 632, Islam spread to other lands. Arab traders and armies took Islam to the rest of the Arabian Peninsula, west into Egypt and Iraq, and north into Syria. Muslim rulers eventually expanded the empire into Persia (now Iran), northern Africa, Spain, and Turkey. Muslim traders took Islam as far east as India, China, and Indonesia.

Below: The Dome of the Rock was built in Jerusalem from 688 to 691. It is the oldest Islamic monument still standing.

European Science

About 150 years before Islam began, the Roman Empire in Western Europe ended. Latin was spoken and written across the Roman Empire. Romans had translated Greek writings into Latin. This allowed scholars in Europe to read Ancient Greek texts. Latin was still used, especially by the Christian Church. Those who worked for the Church copied historic books. This kept much of the ancient learning safe. However, the Church did not encourage science. Christian leaders in Europe often punished scientists whose findings were in conflict with religious teachings.

Expanding Horizons

During Muhammad's life, few Arabs could read. The religion of Islam helped and promoted education. Muhammad's messages from God were written down to make a book called the *Quran*. People wanted to learn to read so they could study the Quran. They also wanted to understand the world, so they read ancient texts written by Greeks and other **scholars**. As Islam spread, its followers gained new knowledge and ideas from different cultures. They used this information to create a unique Islamic style and way of thinking.

Islamic Sacred Sites

This maps show how far the early Islamic Empire had reached by about 750 C.E. Islam had started to spread from the towns of Mecca and Medina in 632. At that time, Arabia was a place of religious diversity. Islam was brought to nearby lands through conquests. First, parts of the Byzantine Empire were conquered. Then, Islamic forces took over much of the Persian (Iranian) Empire.

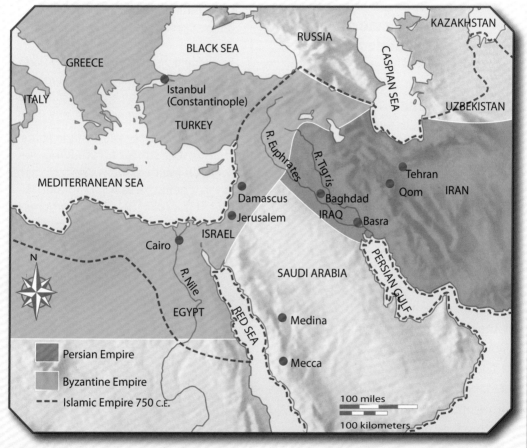

The map highlights many of the cities that became important Islamic centers of learning and education. (Modern city and country names are used.) There was a great exchange of ideas between these centers, and travelers from other parts of Europe and Asia introduced new ways of thinking.

Learning and Ideas

Between 632 and about 1200, Muslim scholars studied the writings of other peoples. These peoples included Visigoths, Greeks, Indians, Chinese, Syrians, and Persians. Muslims studied widely, in science, medicine, and other areas. They added many new ideas to the world's knowledge.

Other Cultures

The Greek civilization 1,000 years before Islam had many brilliant thinkers. Pythagoras, Euclid, and Archimedes were masters of mathematics. Galen, Hippocrates, and Dioscorides wrote about medicine and the human body. Aristotle studied the natural world, including animals and plants. The astronomer Ptolemy wrote about the stars and planets. The Romans, too, had added to science: Pliny the Elder wrote about natural history.

New ideas also came from Asia in the East. The Chinese made such inventions as kites, paper, and clocks. In India, Brahmagupta and Aryabhata had interesting new ideas in mathematics, and Sushruta wrote about surgery.

Muslims knew that they could learn from others by studying a variety of texts. They began what is now known as the "translation movement."

Paper-making

In 751, Muslim soldiers defeated the Chinese at the Battle of Talas River, in central Asia. Among the Chinese soldiers taken prisoner were some who knew the secret of making paper. The prisoners were taken to the Muslim city of Samarkand (in modern Uzbekistan), and made to show people there the secret.

Below: Muslim astronomers made some of the first **observatories** for studying the stars. Following their ideas, the Indian ruler Jai Singh II built this Jantar Mantar in Delhi in 1724. It is a collection of instruments for studying the Sun, Moon, and planets.

Above: An early Islamic illustration shows the physician Ibn Sina (980–1037) seated, preparing a treatment for a patient with smallpox, seen on the right.

Thousands of documents were translated, or copied and rewritten, into Arabic, the language of Islam. Arabic became the new language of learning.

Search For Texts

For a long period of early Islamic history, rulers asked merchants and travelers to seek out books and writings from other lands. They were requested to bring back any information that would add to Islamic knowledge of the world.

House of Wisdom

Muslim leaders that succeeded (came after) Muhammed were called *caliphs*. During the Abbasid Caliphate (750–1258), the caliphs al-Mansur and Harun al-Rashid made Baghdad a major center of knowledge. The city was a peaceful meeting place for different peoples. In the early 800s, caliph Al-Mamun expanded the "House of Wisdom." It was a place for translating, studying, and keeping safe foreign texts. It had observatories to study the stars. It became a famous center for mathematics, alchemy, astronomy, geography, medicine, and other subjects.

As the fame of the House of Wisdom spread, Muslim, Jewish, and Christian scientists traveled there to work together. Similar centers were started in other parts of the Muslim world.

Women As Scholars

Although most of the famous Muslim scholars were men, women also made their mark, especially in studies of law and religion. The university of al-Azhar in Cairo held classes just for female students. One Muslim traveler listed 1,400 of his teachers that included about 80 women. Female students and teachers show up in Islamic university records from early times. Karima al-Marwaziyya in the 1000s and Fatima bint Ibrahim ibn Jowhar in the 1200s were respected teachers of the *hadith*. Shaykha Shuhda was a college lecturer and teacher in Baghdad.

Education

The Quran made it clear that learning about everyday life, nature, and the environment was a duty. Children learned to read by memorizing the Quran. Then at school they learned the words of Muhammad through the religious stories of the **hadiths**. They learned to write Arabic and study the teachings of Islam. By the year 1100, scholars had set up **madrasas**, which were advanced schools for older students. Students could study such subjects as Islamic law and religion, literature, medicine, and astronomy.

A number of Islamic universities were also established. Important ones were in great cities such as Baghdad (Iraq), Cordoba (Spain), Cairo (Egypt), and Delhi (India). Large numbers of students studied mathematics, medicine, astronomy, chemistry, physics, architecture, philosophy, and other subjects.

Texts

Muslims valued books highly. They set up libraries in schools, colleges, and other places of learning. Some people had book collections in their homes and, over time, many mosques had libraries, too. During the 800s, the Islamic library in Baghdad, for example, had thousands of books. No library in Europe had as many books as this until 400 years later. Probably the best library in **medieval** Europe had little more than 1,000 books.

Above: This illustration from a Islamic manuscript of the 1200s shows the Ancient Greek Aristotle (seated) teaching science to students. Everyone is dressed as though they are Muslims.

Three of the largest Islamic libraries were at Baghdad's House of Wisdom, the Fatimid library in Egypt, and the library of the Umayyad in Cordoba, Spain.

From Arabic To Latin

Islamic translators and **scribes**, or recorders, copied Greek and Persian texts into Arabic. In this way, ancient texts reached Europe during the medieval and the **Renaissance** periods of history. Jewish and Christian scholars translated the Arabic into Latin, a language that European scholars could read. Without this passing on of ideas, Europeans would not have learned from the older civilizations. Great European scientists, artists, and scholars, such as Galileo Galilei and Leonardo da Vinci, might not have made the advances they did.

Medicine

The Quran taught Muslims to care for the poor and needy. Care of the sick was the duty of every good Muslim. Over the centuries, sick people in the Islamic world were helped by the Islamic quest for knowledge and by medical advances made by Muslim doctors.

Below: This picture, from a translation of Ibn Sina's *The Canon of Medicine* from the 1200s, shows physicians caring for the sick.

European Medicine

In Europe during the height of Islamic power, medical care was poor. Christians often saw disease as a punishment from God for people's sins. Many medicines were strange mixtures of folk remedies and superstition. Medicine became a serious study after old Greek writings and new Islamic medical texts were translated into Latin and shared across Europe.

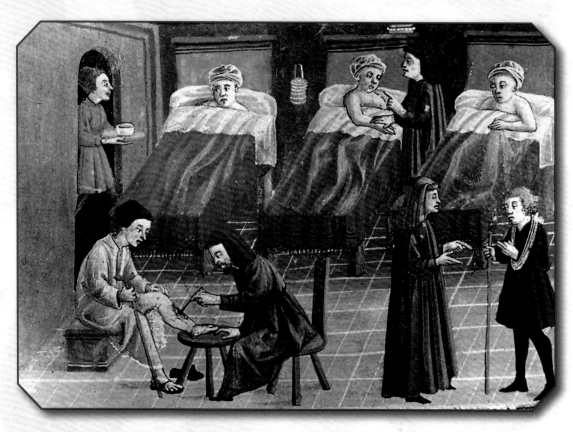

Hospitals

Muslim rulers gave money to build hospitals. The most important hospitals in the Islamic Empire were in Cairo and Damascus. Hospitals were used mostly by poor people and travelers. They gave food, shelter, and medicine to patients. Hospitals had separate sections for men and women.

Physicians

Physicians gave advice on health as well as curing people. Ibn Sina was a scholar, physician, and **polymath** of the early 1000s. His best-known work was called *The Canon of Medicine*. It was translated into Latin and used by doctors as a textbook up to the 1500s.

Al-Razi, or Rhazes, was a doctor and director of Baghdad's hospital. He wrote more than 200 books on medicine. A Jewish physician and philosopher named Maimonides (1135–1204) treated both Jews and Muslims. He even treated Saladin, a Muslim leader.

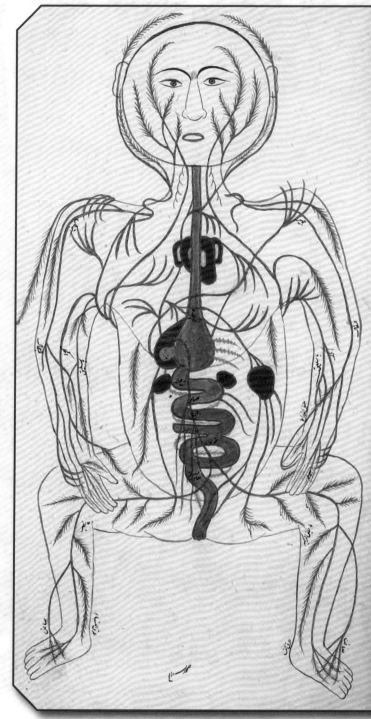

Right: An Islamic anatomical drawing of 1379. It shows the heart, arteries, digestive system, and the kidneys within an outline of the human body.

بنه شفائى دهذ که معاودت صورت نبندذ ومن بحکم این مقدمات از علم طب نبر آن موأم قى

Above: A Muslim physician examines a patient at home.
The illustration is from an Islamic manuscript from the 1300s.

Anatomy

Muslim doctors knew it was important to learn how the human body worked. Yet it seems they rarely dissected, or cut up, bodies to see for themselves the organs inside. For knowledge of the body, they relied mostly on the writings of Galen—a Greek doctor of around the year 200.

Galen believed that oxygen-poor blood went directly between chambers or spaces on either side of the heart. A Muslim doctor named Ibn al-Nafis studied Galen's writings as well as Ibn Sina's *The Canon of Medicine*. In his own text, Ibn al-Nafis described how blood travels from the heart's right ventricle, or lower chamber, to the lungs, then back to the heart's left ventricle. It was 250 years later that European doctors realized this fact about blood circulation.

Pharmacology

Muslim scientists collected and studied writings about herbs and medicines useful for treating diseases and wounds. This is the science of pharmacology. The scientists were interested in the works of doctors such as the Greek Dioscorides, who wrote an encyclopedia around the year 80 showing how plants could be used in medicines. The Islamic world produced some of the first **pharmacists**. They worked alongside doctors. By the early 800s, there were pharmacies in Baghdad.

Mental Illness

Most Muslim doctors saw mental illness as a sickness, needing treatment at home or in a hospital. Elsewhere, mentally ill people were often locked up. Like other peoples at the time, Muslims believed that mental illness was caused by an imbalance in the body's four "humors." Humors were fluids—black and yellow bile, blood, and phlegm.

Islamic hospitals had separate wards for treating patients suffering from dizziness, seizures, headaches, and despair. Physicians thought these were symptoms of mental illness.

Cupping To Help Blood Flow

Below: In parts of the world, cupping is still practiced.

Cupping was a treatment used by Muslim doctors to improve blood circulation. The air inside a small jar was warmed. The jar was then placed tightly against the patient's skin. The cooling air soon created a suction effect within the jar. The pressure sucked the skin in toward the jar, drawing blood to the area. Repeating this over an area increased blood flow.

Surgery

From about 900, Muslims were regularly performing surgery— and with much success. Surgery involves using instruments to cut open, explore, and repair the body.

Types of Surgery

Surgeons in Islamic societies treated wounds, and other skin problems such as boils. They operated on patients to remove bladder stones and treat varicose veins. Surgeons carried out caesarian sections to help women with difficult births. They "bled" patients, which involved cutting a vein to release blood.

Muslim Surgeons

Abu al-Qasim al-Zahrawi (also called Abulcasis) was perhaps the most important Muslim surgeon of his time. He tried out new treatments and methods. He wrote about them in the first known Islamic work on surgery. This text— translated as *The Method of Medicine*— includes a chapter with sketches of instruments and methods. It was used for 800 years to teach Islamic and European surgeons. A 15th-century Turkish surgeon, Serafeddin Sabuncuoglu, translated and added to Zahrawi's text on surgery to create his famous book *Imperial Surgery*.

Like most people at that time, Muslim doctors believed that "bad" blood made a person ill, and so had to be removed.

Dental surgeons took out bad teeth. Eye surgeons removed cataracts, which are a clouding of the lens that creates blurred vision. Other surgeons set broken bones to help them heal.

Muslim surgeons rarely operated deep inside the body. They did not want the patient to get a fatal infection. Just like surgeons today, Muslim surgeons needed the written consent of the patient or patient's family before an operation.

Surgical Instruments

Many instruments, or tools, used by Muslim surgeons were much like those used today. Abulcasis used about 200 surgical instruments, including scalpels for cutting and scraping, scissors, needles for delicate eye operations, saws, forceps, syringes, and splints. Surgeons used cat gut, wool, horse hair, and silk as thread for sutures, or stitches to repair cuts.

Anesthesia

Surgeons used anesthetics to numb areas of the body so patients did not feel pain. Useful painkilling drugs were mandrake, hemlock, Indian hemp, and opium. Opium is still used as an anesthetic.

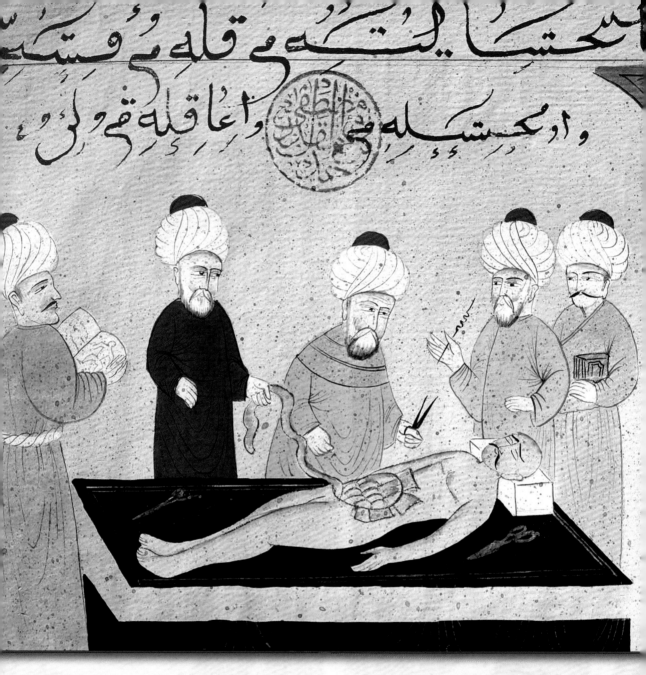

One method used by Muslim doctors was to soak a sponge in a liquid form of the drug and hold it under the patient's nose. Muslim surgeons were the first to describe patients inhaling, or breathing in, anesthetics. They may have been the first to use anesthetics this way.

Above: An Islamic medical encyclopedia illustration from the 1500s shows a team of surgeons performing an operation on a man's intestines.

Alchemy

Ancient alchemy was a mix of science and magic. Alchemists studied natural materials, trying to change one thing into another. They used fire to melt metals, and to make ceramics and glass. They also hoped to discover a "philosopher's stone"—a material to change lead or another metal into gold. Another goal of alchemists was an "elixir of life" —a drink that gave a person long-lasting youth. Alchemy was the forerunner of modern chemistry.

Experimental Science

Muslim scientists learned about alchemy from ancient Greek writings. By the 800s, scholars were writing about alchemy in Arabic. Jabir ibn Hayyan, known to Europeans as Geber, was an important Islamic alchemist. He wrote about how he had tried to remove "impurities" from materials to turn them to gold. He also tried to make an elixir that would give life to objects, and change one type of plant or animal into another.

Jabir's work gave others much useful knowledge, however. He learned to separate metals from rock, make inks and dyes, concentrate acids, and distill, or purify, liquids.

Above: The Arab alchemist Jabir ibn Hayyan (721–815).

His gold-colored ink was used to **illuminate**, or decorate, valued manuscripts, or hand-written texts. He showed glassmakers how to make better glass. Most importantly, he set out rules for accurately conducting science experiments.

Father of Chemistry

Another alchemist was al-Razi (Rhazes). He was the most free-thinking Muslim philosopher. He studied alchemy before he became a physician. While Jabir's ideas included magic and the influence of the planets, al-Razi was more interested in exact scientific practice. He described his experiments, showing how materials were made and how substances behaved. For this reason, al-Razi is often called the father of modern chemistry.

Above: An English illustration from 1490 shows alchemists at work in a laboratory. They are using aludels to try to create gold from other metals.

Islamic Laboratories

Alchemists used many pieces of laboratory apparatus in their experiments. They made containers for liquids, stands to hold the containers, and very hot ovens called kilns. Muslim alchemists improved older pieces of apparatus, and described some for the first time. They may have invented something known as the aludel. This pear-shaped pot was used to collect liquids that were normally difficult to produce. A solid substance was heated. It turned quickly into a gas and aludels cooled the gas and trapped the liquid.

Vision and Optics

Muslim scientists gained a clear understanding of how the human eye works. They studied eye disorders and diseases, and improved the treatments for them. They also studied the physics of light rays and vision—the science of optics.

Theories of Vision

Before the Islamic Empire, people had different ideas about light and eyesight. One theory was that rays of light went from the eyes toward an object and made it visible. Another idea was that light went from the object to the eyes. Most scientists of earlier times agreed with the first theory. A number of Muslim scientists, however, favored the "object-to-eye" idea. This is close to how scientists today explain vision.

Studying the Eye

Muslim eye specialists wrote about the inside of the eye, and how the eye forms an image of an object. Around 850, Baghdad physician Hunayn ibn Ishaq wrote a textbook with the first description of the parts of the eye. He explained how the eye and brain work together so that a person can see. Ali ibn Isa, a Christian doctor in Baghdad, wrote more about

Cataract Surgery

A cataract is a clouding of the lens, the clear disk behind the iris of the eye. Cataracts may develop as a person ages, or be caused by other factors. A clouded lens lets in less light, so eyesight is poor. Muslim surgeons treated cataracts with a fine needle, to move the cloudy lens out of the way.

this subject around the year 1000. So did Fath al-Din al-Qaysi, chief physician in Cairo during the 1200s. In a book on anatomy, al-Qaysi wrote 17 chapters on the structure of the human eye and eye diseases.

Optics

Ibn al-Haytham (Alhazen) also studied the eye. His experiments went beyond looking at the structure of the eye to wondering about light itself. He wondered how light is bent by water and air, and how it is reflected from mirrors. Alhazen also wanted to understand about the color and speed of light. By combining his understanding of the eye with physics, he was able to explain more clearly how light behaves. He brought mathematics to the study of optics.

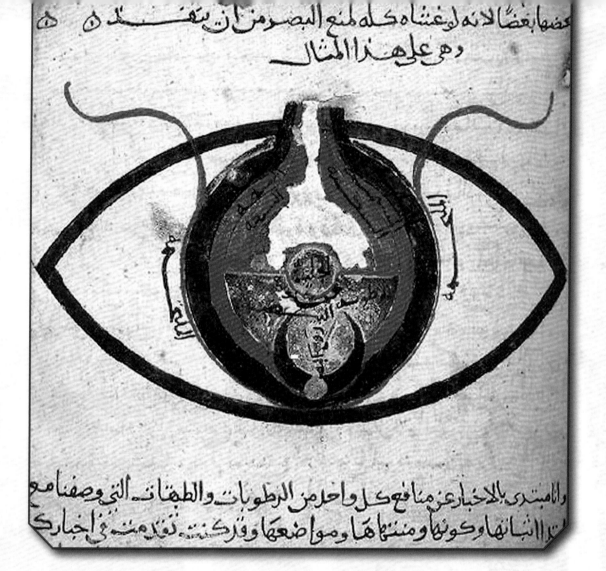

والمبتدى بالاخبار عن منافع كل واحد من الرطوبات والطبقات التي وصفنا مع
انبانها وكونها ومنتها ومواضعها وذكرت تقدم من في اخبارك

The Invention of Eyeglasses

Before the year 100, the Roman scientist Seneca the Younger noted that letters look larger if seen through a glass of water. The Muslim scientist al-Haytham's *Book of Optics* showed how a convex lens such as a glass of water can magnify in this way. In the late 1200s, after his work was translated into Latin, eyeglasses were invented. No one knows who first made them. The eyeglasses had quartz lenses, and rested on the nose. Hundreds of years later, arms to rest on the ears were added to eyeglasses.

Above: This is Hunayn ibn Ishaq's diagram of the eye, as shown in a manuscript from about 1100. It shows blood vessels around the eyeball, the lens (bottom center), and the retina (red area inside).

Astrology and Astronomy

Until the 1000s, Muslim scientists treated astrology and astronomy as one subject. Then they decided that astrology had too much to do with "ungodly forces." Treating astronomy as a science added much to knowledge of the stars and planets.

Astrology

As in other civilizations, many early Muslims thought that the positions of the stars and planets affected people's lives. They believed the stars could foretell events, showing favorable times for surgery, a battle, a journey, or marriage. People paid astrologers to read the star-signs in the **constellations**.

Over time, an increasing number of Muslims thought astrology was more magic than science. Islamic religious

Islamic Calendar

Studying the movement of the Moon and planets helped Muslims mark time. Each Islamic month began on the first day on which the new moon appeared. Calculating this event was important to fix important dates in the calendar.

Left: A picture of the constellation, or star group, known as *Canis Major*, the Great Dog, from a book by Muslim astronomer Al-Sufi.

leaders taught that astrology was wrong. It meant thinking the stars, not God alone, had power over the universe. After the 900s, interest in astrology faded somewhat.

Astronomy

Muslim astronomers knew the works of Indian and Greek astronomers, especially Ptolemy. Ptolemy's star **catalog** listed all the known stars, their sizes, and their positions at different times. From the 800s, Muslim astronomers studied the stars at observatories in Baghdad and other cities. Their observations showed there were problems with some of Ptolemy's theories. They put forward new ideas to explain the motion of stars and planets. Al-Sufi, a Persian astronomer of the 900s, criticized Ptolemy's catalog in a book much studied by European and Arabic scientists. Centuries later, Ibn al-Shatir created an important new model of the ways the planets moved through space.

Supernova

In 1006, a star exploded in the Milky Way galaxy. It was a **supernova**, the brightest ever recorded. It was seen by many people. One of the few who wrote of what they saw was 18-year-old Egyptian stargazer Ibn Ridwan. He wrote about the supernova's brightness and the position of the Moon and planets at the time. This helped modern astronomers to find evidence of the supernova.

Muslim astronomers drew up a new calendar. It was based on the lunar (Moon) cycle, not the solar (Sun) cycle. Day one of the Islamic era was the day in 622 when Muhammad started the *hijra* or migration from Mecca to Medina. That year became the point from which the Islamic calendar started.

Above: This book illustration from 1557 shows Ottoman astronomers using a range of scientific equipment in an **observatory**.

Military Science

Early Muslim soldiers used the weapons of their times. In battles, they fought with spears, daggers, and swords. In a siege they used artillery or throwing weapons to knock holes in fortress walls. By fighting and defeating other peoples, Muslims learned about and improved new weapons and different battle techniques.

Weapons

Islamic artillery weapons were like large catapults. The *mangonel* was a giant sling for throwing heavy rocks. During the 1400s, al-Zaradkash wrote an Islamic military manual called *An Elegant Book*

Damascus Swords

From the 900s to the 1400s, the most prized swords were made in Damascus in Syria. They were made in a still-unknown process of forging steel that created patterns like flowing water. Most had a curved blade, and were known as scimitars. They were made for slashing rather than thrusting. In Europe, people called any fine sword a Damascus sword, even if it was not made in Damascus.

Below: Krak des Chevaliers in northern Syria was a castle used by Christians and Muslims during the Crusades. It came under siege and was captured by Muslims in 1271.

on Mangonels. He described older, forgotten designs of this weapon, with instructions on how to build and use them.

For defense, lightweight but powerful catapults were placed on the walls of Islamic fortresses. Christian armies in Spain began using such weapons, too.

Another siege weapon was the *ziyar,* a type of bow. Some ziyars were small enough that four would fit on an ox-drawn wagon. A giant ziyar needed 20 men to draw back its bowstring to fire big arrows.

Flaming Weapons

In the 600s, Muslim armies began using "Greek fire." This was a fire-bomb, made from oil mixed with other materials, that was flung at the enemy. The flames of the fire-bomb were hard to put out. Islamic soldiers used Greek fire to burn the wooden siege weapons used by **Crusaders**. By the year 1000, Muslims were adding saltpeter, an explosive ingredient used in gunpowder. This made Greek fire even more destructive.

Above: This painting from Iran in the 1400s shows armor and weapons used by Islamic cavalry—warriors on horseback.

The dry climate of the Middle East and North Africa spurred advances in machines to aid farmers and bring water to towns. Levers, gears, and waterwheels had been invented long before the Islamic era, but Islamic engineers improved such devices. They used them in new ways for local needs.

Waterwheels

Many Muslims lived in arid lands, where machines able to scoop up, move, and harness precious water were useful and often essential. Islamic engineers perfected waterwheels that could scoop up water from ditches for irrigation, the artificial watering of farmland. They developed other waterwheels that could

Right: An illustration from Islamic engineer Al-Jazari's *The Book of Knowledge of Ingenious Mechanical Devices*. The book was published around 1205. The illustration shows a musical machine that dispenses drinks. It is not known whether such a machine was ever built and worked.

use the power of flowing water along rivers to turn machinery. The machines were used to grind grain to make flour, crush sugar cane, or saw lumber for furniture and building construction.

Clocks

Mechanical clocks, often powered by flowing water, were used before the Islamic era. Muslims copied old clock designs and improved them. In the 1000s, al-Zarqali built a water clock in Toledo, Spain. At the end of the 1100s, an engineer named al-Jazari wrote about fountains, and about water- and candle-clocks. The clocks in al-Jazari's book were more complex and delicate than previous clocks.

Automatons

Some of al-Jazari's machines had many moving parts. He used the technology to make moving figures, worked by sets of gear wheels. Such clever devices led to such later inventions as chiming clocks, combination locks, and even the robots of modern times.

Flights of Fancy

As well as automatons, Muslims liked to have fun with mechanical toys. Inventors made birds that could whistle and sing. Such toys amused rich rulers at home and in their gardens. The toys were water-driven or worked by sets of gears. Some children's pedal-cars today are based on the designs.

Left: Al-Jazari's design for a water pump. Animal power was used to turn gears. These were linked to a pump that forced water upward from a river.

Green Revolution

Soon after Muslim armies had conquered territories, Muslim officials moved in. They started to tax local farmers and to look for ways to improve farm output. Muslim farmers followed, introducing crops from their homelands. These required different methods of farming.

Wind Power and Cooling

Strong winds can wither crops, uproot trees, and sink small boats. Muslim engineers, however, made use of wind power in machines. They built many windmills. The wind turned sails and, as the sails turned, they drove a large wheel inside the mill. A windmill could draw up groundwater for crops, press olives to extract their oil, or turn a heavy millstone to grind grain.

Wind was also used to ventilate and cool buildings. Many buildings, especially in Persia and around the Gulf, had a wind tower or wind catcher on top. Some also had a water reservoir underneath and fountains inside. The buildings were designed to keep people inside cool, with a flow of fresh air through the rooms.

Right: This wind tower is in Arabia. Wind towers and wind catchers have been used here for centuries. They are useful for cooling buildings in regions where it gets very hot during the day. A network of openings and vents catches and draws air into and around the rooms of a building. Stale, warm air is pushed out of the building.

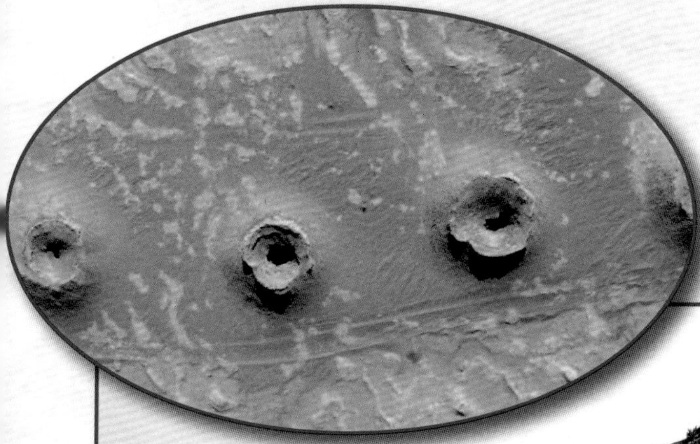

Left: A view from the air of dry land shows three openings of vertical shafts from a qanat, an underground water channel.

Above: This ancient aqueduct, or water channel, built across a river (seen here dried up) was used to direct water toward the town of Yazd in present-day Iran.

Carrying Water

Muslim traders took plants to conquered lands. In this way, new types of crops were spread through the empire. Often, a new farm crop needed more water than was available naturally. Irrigation was the answer. Farmers had watered fields long before Muhammad's lifetime, but Muslim engineers improved irrigation methods. They restored old dams and built new dams to store water.

Muslim engineers also used *qanats*, or sloping underground water channels.

Qanats were built before Islamic times to carry water beneath the surface from mountains to arid plains. Qanats helped farmers to grow crops on land that before had been too dry. They could also help gardeners raise flowers, and cultivate lush palace gardens. Muslims introduced qanats into Spain and North Africa.

Mathematics

Muslim mathematicians developed new ways of counting and writing numbers based on ideas from Ancient Greece. They even changed the numbers themselves— to those we use today. Advances in mathematics led to many of the modern ways of doing math. The word algebra comes from the Arabic *al-jabr,* meaning a way to solve equations.

Numbers

The numbers 1 through 9 used in North America today are a combination of **Hindu** and Islamic numerals, or number symbols. Muslim mathematicians changed the shapes of the numerals from India. They used numbers widely in daily life, especially in trade and science.

Indian mathematicians first had the idea of "place-value"—figures being placed into the units, tens, and hundreds columns, for example. Muslim mathematicians did the same. They also added the numeral 0 to the nine Hindu numbers to represent the concept of zero.

Muslim Mathematicians

Al-Khwarizmi was a mathematician who lived in Baghdad in the 800s. His most famous written work was *Algebra.*

Above: Early Islamic tile patterns, like this one from Uzbekistan, were designed using skills in geometry that were not matched by those in the West for more than 500 years.

It is about solving equations. Another of his books describes the use of the new Arabic numbers, the so-called "notation of Al-Khwarizmi." In Europe, this became "algorithm," a modern math term.

Omar Khayyam, known as "the tentmaker," was another famous Muslim mathematician. He advanced the study of geometry (see page 32) and found new ways to solve quadratic equations, which can find the values of unknown variables.

Below: A diagram by Ibn al-Haytham (see page 20) showing the use of mathematics in optics. Arabic letters are used as markers.

see page 32

Using Math

Math had many practical uses in the Islamic Empire. Astronomers calculated angles to measure the height of a star above the horizon, for navigation. Artists used geometry to create mosaics. Math helped Muslims to fix the correct times to pray, and know in which direction to turn to pray facing Mecca. Math was also used for fun and magic "charms." Muslims invented the "magic square"—a square of numbers in which rows, columns, and diagonals each add to the same number.

Geometry

Geometry is about points and lines, angles, and shapes and surfaces. The Islamic study of this key branch of mathematics began in the 800s when a geometry textbook by the Greek Euclid was translated into Arabic. By the 900s, Muslim scientists were questioning some of Euclid's ideas. They studied cones and other complex geometric shapes. In the 1100s, the Jewish scholar Savasorda wrote about Arabic geometry in Hebrew, spreading new ideas to Spain.

Left: This is an astrolabe from the 1400s used by travelers to help them navigate, or find their way. Markers on the instrument are lined up with a star or planet and figures read off one of the scales.

Trigonometry

Trigonometry is the geometry of the relationships between the sides and angles of triangles. Spherical trigonometry is used to work out the angles of triangles that form the sides of a section of a sphere. Its study was important because it helped Muslim scientists fix the positions of the Sun and Moon in the sky, to work out the dates of holy days. Al-Khwarizmi was an early expert in spherical trigonometry.

The Math of Navigation

By using math, travelers at sea or in the desert could measure how far they had journeyed and in what direction. They did so by comparing the height of a planet or star in the sky on different nights. An instrument called an **astrolabe** helped travelers fix a star's position. That way, they could figure out where they were. For trade caravans crossing deserts or merchant ships at sea, such knowledge was vital.

Left: An illustration from a Turkish manuscript from about 1500 shows a type of six-ringed armillary sphere. The thin string with a weight at the end (in the center) was a pendulum used to make sure the instrument was kept perfectly upright.

Armillary Spheres

The Ancient Greeks made models of the planets' movements, or orbits, to teach astronomy. The models were spheres made of rings, with each ring showing the path of a planet or star. Models with lots of rings were known as armillary spheres. Using spherical trigonometry, Muslim scientists were able to study the movements and orbits of several planets, stars, and the Moon. This helped them to understand the constellations, or groupings of stars, and to keep an accurate calendar. It also influenced where and how they built observatories with telescopes to study the night sky.

Islamic traders traveled widely, and Muslims who could afford to were expected to travel at least once to the holy city of Mecca. Religious writings also encouraged seafaring. As Islam spread, Muslim scientists made navigational instruments such as the astrolabe. Muslim geographers created accurate maps of the places they visited.

The Study of Geography

In Baghdad's House of Wisdom, some of the works copied from Greek, Persian, and Hindu were books about geography. In them were numerous mistaken ideas, such as the idea that the Indian Ocean was enclosed by land. Other information was more reliable. Scholars from Iran shared the idea of describing the world by compass points: East, West, North, and South.

There were two major early Islamic schools of geography. Students of the Iraqi school wrote geography texts based on exploration. The Balkhi school students used countries as a way to divide up the world when describing it. They also wrote about the languages, customs, and beliefs of people in various areas. The Balkhi scholars are thought to be the first to use **perspective**—a sense of depth—in maps.

Below: Al-Idrisi's world map from the 1100s, showing Africa at the top and Europe below.

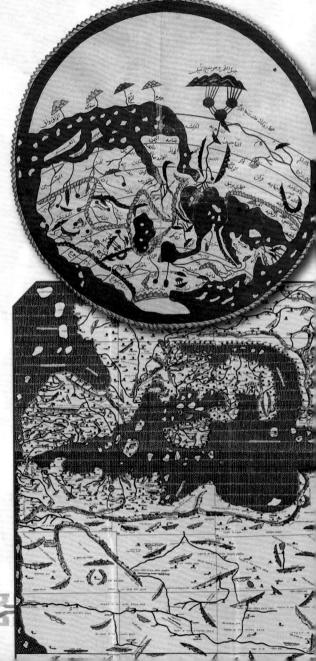

Cartography

Muslim cartographers, or map-makers, created more accurate and detailed maps than those produced in medieval Europe. While not as accurate as modern maps, the Islamic maps clearly show how people thought of the world at that time. Muslim cartographers kept very busy too, for there are thousands of their maps in collections around the world.

Al-Idrisi

In the 1100s, Roger II of Normandy, France, took control of Sicily. He made the Mediterranean island a center for cultured Muslims and Christians. Roger was very interested in geography, and invited the famous Muslim cartographer al-Idrisi to Sicily to work for him. During a 16-year stay, al-Idrisi made a number of maps, and also a type of encyclopedia of the world as it was known to him.

Islamic Atlases

From the 900s, maps were sometimes added to bigger printed works. Such books were like a modern atlas. They included discussions about the world, such as why some peoples were darker-skinned than others. Books about countries and people often included a world map, along with maps of regions. Atlas-type books were popular for hundreds of years, and they still are now.

Below: The *Tabula Rogeriana* is al-Idrisi's world map from 1154, made for King Roger II of Sicily. It combines 70 separate maps.

Below: This picture from about 1860 shows Ibn Battuta in Egypt on one of his many journeys.

Ibn Battuta

Ibn Battuta was a record-breaking Muslim traveler. This scholar, judge, and explorer spent his life making journeys all over the world. He often acted as an ambassador for local rulers he met on the way. One journey lasted 24 years. At the order of a Moroccan ruler, a scribe named Ibn Juzayy wrote a book about Ibn Battuta's travels. *Journey of Ibn Battuta* is mostly accurate, but with a little exaggeration.

Explorers

Several explorers traveled through Muslim lands and beyond. In the 900s, the Jewish merchant Ibrahim ibn Yaqub journeyed from Spain to Germany. Spanish traveler Ibn Jubayr made three long journeys. Unfortunately, when such travelers brought home descriptions of distant places, new facts were not often added to European maps. Also, if what explorers described did not fit existing ideas about world geography, new information was often rejected.

The great Muslim explorer Ibn Battuta was born in Morocco in 1304. He made many amazing journeys. He traveled from Spain in the west to Indonesia in the east, and from Africa in the south to Europe in the north. He spent nine years in India. The story of his travels is usually just called the *Journey of Ibn Battuta*. It remained unknown in the West until the 1800s, when it was rediscovered by French historians.

Modes of Travel

The camel is the ideal animal for travel in the deserts of Arabia. A camel is tough, can walk across hot sand and rock, and go for days without food. It stores fat in its hump to nourish it when food is scarce. A camel's body can absorb heat without perspiring and losing precious water. Camels were used to carry people as well as goods. Caravans, or processions, of camels, rather than wagons, were used by Muslim traders on long land trips.

Muslim sailors used various types of craft. Some were small boats for coastal trips. Others were sailing ships so large that they carried smaller boats for use when visiting ports. Merchant ships were made in special designs to carry different cargoes. Cargo ships were at least three times wider than their height, so they would not easily roll over in rough seas.

Below: This picture from an atlas from 1375 shows European merchants meeting Ibn Battuta's caravan on their way to China.

Scholars

In the early Islamic world, education and learning were highly regarded. As ancient texts were translated, ideas from far and wide were passed on. Fields of study were not separated as they are today, so many Muslim scholars were polymaths with skills in many subjects. Here are some of the most famous.

Al-Kindi about 801–873

Al-Kindi wrote about philosophy, geography, politics, physics, mathematics, meteorology, music, optics, alchemy, and astrology. He is considered the founder of Islamic philosophy. His writings on how people see led to the rules of perspective applied during the European Renaissance.

Ibn Ishaq about 809–873

A famous translator in Baghdad was Hunayn Ibn Ishaq, also known as Jannitus. He traveled widely looking for interesting texts. A skilled physician, he wrote texts on nutrition, philosophy, astronomy, mathematics, and optics.

Above: Scholars discuss philosophy in Baghdad's House of Wisdom, Islam's first important institute of learning from the 800s to the 1200s.

Ibn Al-Haytham
about 965–1040

Ibn al-Haytham (Alhazen) spent much of his life in Egypt. He wrote more than 90 works on astronomy, mathematics, optics, logic, politics, poetry, and music. Some think his *Book of Optics* is the most important work in Islamic science.

Al-Biruni
about 973–1048

Abu Rayhan al-Biruni wrote nearly 150 works on astronomy, mathematics, cartography, philosophy, literature, medicine, and history. He helped pass on some Indian mathematical ideas, but little else of his work reached Europe since his writings were never translated into Latin.

Ibn Sina
about 980–1037

Known in Europe as Avicenna, this Muslim physician was one of the great thinkers of his time. He was famous as a mathematician, philosopher, poet, and politician. He wrote about many subjects. For example, he studied energy in its various forms. His book *The Canon of Medicine* was an important advance in the progress of science.

Right: An engraving of Ibn Sina, who argued that reason and religion can work together.

Sons of Musa

In the mid-800s, three brothers known as the *Banu Musa* [Sons of Musa], studied in Baghdad and became important scientists for Caliph al-Mamun. They spent their money collecting old documents and having them translated. They also wrote books themselves, on astronomy, mathematics, and engineering. The brothers calculated Earth's circumference at 24,000 miles (38,624 kilometers). This is only 900 miles (1,448 km) less than today's accepted distance.

If Muslim scholars had not translated and expanded on ancient texts, much knowledge might have been lost. Scribes translated many old books from Greek and other languages into Arabic, then Latin. Latin was the common language of learning within the Western, or Christian, world. Without this work, European Renaissance scholars would not have had the scientific background for their new ideas.

Arabic Words

Many ideas from the Islamic world affected non-Muslims, who had regular contacts with Muslim traders and merchants. Islamic ideas helped to shape European thought and the modern world. For example, here are some scientific words that have their roots in Arabic culture—alchemy, alcohol, algebra, algorithm, alkali, amalgam, borax, camphor, chemistry, elixir, zenith, and zero. Many terms for parts of the body come from Arabic as well, including aorta, cornea, diaphragm, and pancreas.

Libraries

During the Islamic Empire, libraries were not just "treasure houses of books," which is a translation of an Arabic word for a library. They were also places of learning, in the way schools and universities are today. From the 1000s, libraries were often part of colleges of higher learning, or madrasas. Al-Azhar in Cairo, Egypt, was a mosque with its own library. The library in Cordoba,

Right: Tulip flowers in bloom. The name *tulip* comes from a Persian word used to describe the shape of turbans worn by some Arabs.

Spain, had more than one million volumes and welcomed students of all religions and origins. In general, Islamic libraries valued learning for its own sake.

Paper

When Muslims improved paper-making, they changed history. Making more paper more cheaply allowed an increase in the number of books produced. More ancient handwritten manuscripts were translated and copied. The widespread use of paper allowed a wider access to books, especially after the invention of the printing press in Europe in the 1400s.

Below: Doctors examine a urine specimen from the ailing Duke of Normandy in France in about 1350. Medical practices such as this spread across Europe from the Islamic world and led to the building of many hospitals.

Biographies

Here are short biographies of some of the key scientists, physicians, and mathematicians of the early Islamic world. In time, their thoughts, ideas, and inventions would greatly influence Western culture and East Asian culture.

Al-Mansur 714–775

In 765, Abu Jafar al-Mansur founded Baghdad as a cultural and political center. He was the first ruler to have books translated into Arabic, preparing the way for the "House of Wisdom" in Baghdad (see page 10).

Right: A picture of the physician al-Razi. His full name was Abu-Bakr Muhammad ibn-Zakariya al-Razi.

Harun Al-Rashid 763–809

The reign of the Abbasid caliph al-Rashid is often called Islam's Golden Age. He gave support to the "House of Wisdom" and its work in the sciences and arts. Al-Rashid is often used as the caliph in stories from *One Thousand and One (Arabian) Nights*.

Al-Khwarizmi
about 780–850

Al-Khwarizmi's book on mathematics led to algebra. He also helped create the numerals used in modern times. The mathematical term "algorithm" comes from his name.

Al-Razi 864–930

Also known as Rhazes, al-Razi started out as an alchemist and became a respected Baghdad physician. His studies of the diseases smallpox and measles form the basis of modern hygiene.

Al-Sufi 903–986

This astronomer, also called Azophi, identified some of the first galaxies outside of Earth's Milky Way. His catalog of stars and constellations was used for centuries. A Moon crater and a star are named for him.

Al-Zahrawi 936–1013

Al-Zahrawi, also called Abulcasis, was a physician in Spain. He wrote a 30-volume encyclopedia of medicine, covering subjects ranging from anatomy to making surgical tools.

Omar Khayyam 1048–1131

Omar Khayyam did physics research and built a water balance. He is most famous for his poetry, his work on mathematics, and improving the accuracy of the lunar calendar.

Savasorda 1070–1145

This Jewish scholar, whose real name was Abraham bar Hiyya ha-Nasi, wrote in Hebrew about Islamic science, including geometry, algebra, and trigonometry. His writings were translated into Latin, which made it possible for Europeans to read about Arabic mathematics.

Right: A manuscript illumination from about 1350 for a translation of Al-Sufi's star catalog from about 964.

Ibn Jubayr 1145–1217

This explorer's first journey spanned two years and took him to Sicily, Greece, Egypt, Iraq, Syria, and Palestine. His writings contain much information about everyday life in the places he visited.

Ibn Al-Nafis 1213–1288

The physician Ibn al-Nafis wrote medical works, though many were lost for centuries. His accurate explanation of the circulation of blood through the heart and lungs was rediscovered only in 1924.

Ibn Al-Shatir 1304–1375

Like other astronomers, Ibn al-Shatir drew up tables to list and catalog the stars and their movements across the sky. With his knowledge, he worked out the exact dates for Islamic holy days and times for daily prayers. He built astronomical instruments, and his planetary model was an improvement on that of Greek astronomer Ptolemy.

The Extent of the Early Islamic World

Early Muslim merchants, traders, and armies took their faith, customs, and learning across the world. From the 600s, Islam spread out from the Arabian Peninsula into the Middle East, northern Africa, and southern Europe, and also reached parts of East Asia and Southeast Asia. This map shows areas that were under Muslim rulers after the first main conquests (up to the year 750), then at the end of the Ottoman Empire. Islamic science, medicine, and mathematics enriched the world and set the stage for the progress of the European Renaissance, or rebirth of ideas, from about 1350 to 1600.

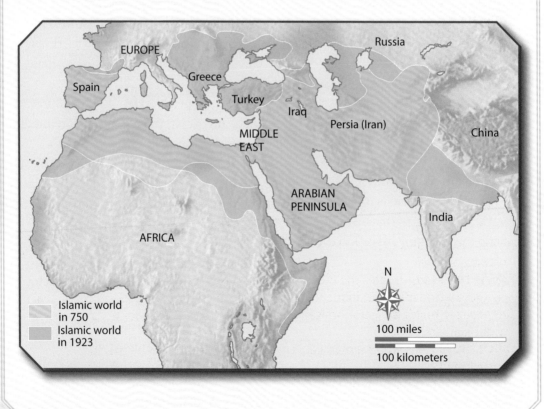

EUROPE

Russia

Spain

Greece

Turkey

Iraq

Persia (Iran)

China

MIDDLE EAST

ARABIAN PENINSULA

India

AFRICA

N

Islamic world in 750
Islamic world in 1923

100 miles

100 kilometers

Early Islamic World

Key dates in Science, Medicine, Math

622 Islamic era begins

705 First basic Islamic hospital opens, in Damascus

751 Muslims learn paper-making

775 Ancient manuscripts begin to be translated

828 Astronomical observatory built in Baghdad

830 "House of Wisdom" started in Baghdad

830 Al-Khwarizmi writes about algebra and Hindu-Arabic numerals

about 850 Hunayn ibn Ishaq describes the workings of the human eye

960s Al-Sufi writes about the stars

970 First university, al-Azhar, is founded in Cairo

1006 Ibn Ridwan writes about seeing a supernova

1012–1021 Ibn al-Haytham makes an early type of camera

before 1037 Ibn Sina writes *The Canon of Medicine*

before 1038 Ibn al-Haytham writes his *Book of Optics*

1138–1154 Al-Idrisi creates the most accurate world maps yet made

1206 Al-Jazari builds an astronomical water-powered clock

about 1280 Al-Nafis writes a medical encyclopedia

1325 Ibn Battuta begins his first journey

Rest of the World

Key dates in Science, Medicine, Math

674 Chinese atlas of stars is created

731 Bede writes about England's history and religion

900 Medical textbook created in Byzantium from Greek texts from around the year 100

about 950 Latin manuscript written in Spain introduces Islamic astrolabe and Islamic astronomy

1075–1098 Earliest known Western medical text published in Italy. It was written by a Muslim

1119 Chinese author first records the use of a magnetic compass

1200 The abacus, a Chinese adding device, is invented

1202 Italian Fibonacci persuades Europeans to adopt the Arabic number system

1455 The *Gutenberg Bible* is the first book produced on a printing press

1485–1516 Italian polymath and artist Leonardo da Vinci makes accurate anatomical drawings

1494 Italian Luca Pacioli's important mathematics text, including algebra, is written

1519 Ferdinand Magellan sets out to circumnavigate the globe by sea

1564 Nicolaus Copernicus suggests that the planets do not orbit Earth, but instead orbit the Sun

1609 German astronomer Hans Kepler publishes his work on planetary motion

Glossary

Allah The one true God of Islam, from *al* (the) *ilah* (god)

allies People or nations working together

astrolabe A navigational instrument that relies on the position of stars in the sky

catalog A list of items, such as stars, arranged in a logical order

constellations Groups of stars, often given names for their picture-shapes

Crusaders Soldiers who fought against Muslims and were supported by the Catholic Church

Crusades A series of religious wars fought between European Christians and Muslims in Palestine, Egypt, and Turkey

hadith Personal accounts of Muhammad's sayings and behavior

hajj The Muslim pilgrimage to Mecca

hijra The migration of the first Muslims from Mecca to Medina

Hindu Related to Hinduism, the ancient religion of India

illuminate To decorate with colors and illustrations often on a book page

Islam The religion or faith based on God's messages to Muhammad

Kaaba The holiest site in Islam, a square building in Mecca

madrasas Schools for teaching Islamic religion, law, and other subjects

medieval Of the Middle Ages in Europe (roughly from the 500s to the 1400s)

mosque A building used as a Muslim place of worship or house of prayer

Muslim A person who follows the faith of Islam

nomads People with no fixed home, who instead move from place to place

observatory A building equipped with instruments to look at the night sky

Ottoman The Turkish Muslim empire founded about 1300 and ended in 1918

perspective An art technique that gives a flat drawing the illusion of depth

pharmacists People skilled in making medicines

polymath A person with a wide range of knowledge and interests

prophet A religious teacher who was inspired by God, as Muhammad was

Quran Islam's holy book, containing the messages Muhammad said came from God

Renaissance The period of European revival in art, literature, and learning (about 1350 to 1600)

scholar A highly educated person; someone who seeks knowledge

scribes People skilled in reading and writing for others

siege An attack on a city or fortress to make it surrender

supernova A very bright exploding star

translate To rewrite from one language into another

Further Information

Books

Barnard, Bryn. *The Genius of Islam: How Muslims Made the Modern World.* New York: Knopf Books For Young Readers, 2011.

Beshore, George. *Science in Early Islamic Culture.* New York: Franklin Watts, 1998.

Davis, Lucile. *Life During the Great Civilizations: The Ottoman Empire.* San Diego: Blackbirch Press, 2004.

Rumford, James. *Traveling Man: The Journey of Ibn Battuta, 1325–1354.* New York: Houghton Mifflin, 2001.

Spilsbury, Louise, and Richard Spilsbury. *The Islamic Empires* (Time Travel Guides). Bloomington: Raintree, 2007.

Stone, Caroline. *Eyewitness Books: Islam.* New York: Dorling Kindersley, 2005.

Websites

History of Science and Technology in Islam
www.history-science-technology.com

Biography of Al-Khwarizmi
www.mathsisgoodforyou.com/people/alkhwarizmi.htm

1001 Inventions: The Enduring Legacy of Muslim Civilisation
www.1001inventions.com

Videos

Science and Islam, BBC documentary by Jim Al-Khalili, 2009

Islam: Empire of Faith, PBS documentary by Robert Gardner and narrated by Ben Kingsley, 2005

Index